CW00448123

A Mother's Lament

Nikki Rodwell

A Mother's Lament
Index

Note from author

They say the pain of childbirth is made more bearable by the fact it is 'pain with a purpose'. Some of us experience after pains that are equally, if not more, painful. My hope is that these poems will give purpose to that pain. Putting pen to paper is incredibly healing, and I hope others, especially mothers who have grieved in any way or struggled with their relationships, may be touched by some of my words. Remember, that no-one and nothing can strip you of your title.

You are and always will be a mother.

Nine Months

Excitement, fear
As the time draws near
Your heartbeat as mine
From month one til nine

Now ready to meet you
I don't want you to leave
Stay safe in my belly
Don't force me to grieve

Yet no force could stop you
With your birth came a price
The umbilical cord
Cut once
Then twice

A Newborn

Your plump fingers
Curl into mine
Loves tender grip
Innocence divine

HAIKU

A womb nurtures life
released by a severed cord
our sentence begins.

Overboard

I harboured your wriggling body
For nine months
Giving release for your safe passage
From dream to wakefulness

Mid voyage your compass went awry
With the wind in your sails
Your boat threw me overboard

Forced to tread water
Hands clutching to driftwood
I wait for your return

The Generation Game

A white Barbie jeep
      Bunk beds where you sleep
A bear of your choice
      With a tape of mum's voice
A sparkly two-piece
      A peanut-filled Reese
A pink fluffy wand
      A Girls World with hair blonde
A build-your-own rocket
      Fully dressed Polly Pocket

Keep noting them all
      For the test on recall

Mr Frosty no less
His slush puppy's the best
A sea-monkey tank
      Your own piggy bank
Here's a steep marble run
      Some foam discs and a gun
A cabbage patch doll
      A long-haired pink troll
Soft TY Beanies
      Polka dot bikinis

The conveyer belt slows
  With an allowance for clothes

Makeup and scrunchies
  A packet of Munchies
An electric guitar
  For the budding rockstar
Now, who wants to own
  A laptop and iPhone?

The conveyor belt stops
  And the slide door drops

It's over too soon
  The memories strewn
Each item forgotten
  Decaying and rotten
There is no star prize
  Just troubled goodbyes

An Illusory Moment

The perfect picture
a mother holding her child,
both gazing through a window
at the world that awaits them.
She hugs his squirming body
tight to her chest.
He flaps his arms
at a passing bird.
So much to explore,
the world his playground.
She gazes without seeing,
inhaling the powdery freshness
of his untarnished body,
capturing the moment
for her keepsake box.
Her nose rubs his scalp,
placing gentle kisses,
with whispers of love.
Her grip tightens,
desperate

to feel his chubby ringed thighs
for a moment longer,
knowing this moment will fade,
but
blissfully unaware
the frame is cracked,
the picture a fraud,
the moment an illusion.

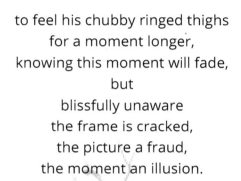

Careful what you wish for

The taxi driver's meter
ticks in the seven-seater,
one day they'll drive themselves
her ferrying days slip by.

The multi-tasking cook
each taste not overlooked,
she believes the day will come
when they'll return for pecan pie.

The seamstress, the teacher,
the voice of a preacher,
hopes that come the future
their lessons will be learnt.

The wiper of tears
who sweeps away their fears,
the storyteller blind
that her fingers will be burnt.

The personal shopper
spends every last copper,
keeping them in fashion
until the day they earn.

The mother's frantic line
'when will time again be mine?'
but alas, once set free,
some are never to return.

BROKEN PIECES

You shun the mother I never
was, finding solace
in cruel punishment,
bestowing me a heart
of broken pieces.

But you were the daughter
I always wanted,
my door left open
hoping you would find me,
until you became
a dangerous stranger.

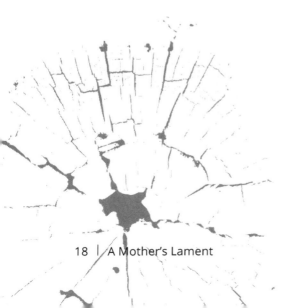

20 mg

A pill can numb the pain

of love forlorn.

Yet it leaves

a brackish aftertaste

my palate flavoured

with shrapnel.

Mother Role

Don't lose yourself

In mother identity

For redundancy

Pays no dividend

Leaving your self-worth

On the breadline

Love Unrequited

The core of a mother
yearning to love 'n' cherish
forsaken by millennial offspring;
an era soon to perish.

AMBIGUOUS LOSS

Rejected by your progeny
mind's logic explodes,
hope splatters on the wall
in permanent ink
like dark bruises that won't fade.

The forever relationship
hangs by tangled cord,
it pulls at my threadbare heart
forcing it to seep fresh blood
through lacerations, made
by their knife-edged words.

Perhaps I should have gouged it out
to gift wrap in bloodied silk,
before it deflated
into dried up nothingness.
But would it have made a difference?

As lies hijack their minds
your existence crumbles;
all that you are, you are not.
A hologram behind frosted glass.

Indifference is more dangerous than hate,
its opposite has no love.
As icy waters seep into my soul,
angry words departed,
numbed tears fill the hole.

Grief for a living child
throws your world out of orbit-
with eyes of a new-born infant
you must learn to live your life
inside out, and upside down.

Blurred Boundaries

Your birthday made me a mother
a title worn with pride,
until you stripped it from me
and a part of me just died.

Your age has nearly doubled
since the day you chose to leave,
my sentence never ending,
your cruel words with no reprieve.

The boundaries of approval,
blurred, forever shifting,
the elusive pot of gold,
my sorrow never lifting.

Words become your weapon,
entitlement your shield,
"be a mother not a victim"
a new title now revealed.

But a mother has their limit,
my sentence has an end,
a murderer gets less punishment
than a mother who's condemned.

Desecration

BEWARE THE PERSON
WHO DEFACES THE PAGE
WITH A BITTER HAND
FOR THE INDELIBLE INK
WILL STAIN
THEIR TAINTED HEART

Lessons in Love

They didn't ask to be born
Blame lies at my door
For those of my creation
Hate deep-down to the core

Did I never teach them
Unconditional love?
To hold respect for elders
Leave judgement to heavens above?

A degree in life has value
But a lesson far more blessed
Love goes hand in hand
With forgiveness manifest

Wasted Years

.... like empty bookshelves

with stories

of love

fading

to ashes.

Clichés

Ignore the small stuff, pick your battles well,

For a teenager's angst will come out
in the wash.

What remains is that which you've earnt;

You reap what you sow.

I was shit at needlework.

Metamorphosis

A woman in vibrant colour

flying with wings of freedom.

A mother in black and white

unrecognisable

her metamorphosis

shunned.

Solo Dance

It takes one to change

and learn different steps

but she will dance alone

to musique obscure

the orchestra plays

a solitary tango

pour deux

I love you, but I don't like you:

If, as a mother,

these words have never left your mouth,

you are truly blessed,

maybe one in a million.

Closing the Door

When you uttered those words
did you not see the flaw?
Saying no crime's too great
to close your front door?

With the door left ajar
you sealed your own fate,
with the unsought intruder
of anger and hate.

It snaked through your home
and tortured your soul
destruction and vengeance
its singular goal.

It nearly took hold
biting deep to the core,
til the day finally came...
and you bolted the door.

A Broken Back

Learning to walk was easy
But without you
My crutches were torn away
Each step taking me to
Nowhere

INCONSISTENT EQUATION

(a) degree to which you want something to be different

=

(b) degree to which you will suffer

Hint: acceptance is the hidden variable

My answer: a + b = headfuck

(some things are too hard to accept)

The Piano

Her fingers show love
In the nocturne she plays
Her concerto more complex
With keys set ablaze

Little Miss Perfect

Climbing great heights
Perfection personified
Looking down on the crop
Where wheat and chaff cried
For neither belonged
In her majestic story
No field of gold
Could crown her glory

You Are My Sunshine

When you retreat behind cloud
I feel your pain as if mine.
When your rays dim,
tis like a sunflower wilting.

Yet behind grey skies
your true nature still shines:
resolute, radical,
ambient light for humanity.

Wherever your journey beckons
you bestow upon this world,
the warmth of your smile,
the kindness in your heart.

Your soul seeks out true love,
as a mother I have found mine;
I see you behind the clouds,
a blessed gift from the Divine.

Drowning in tears

I taste the salt
of tears drenching my soul
relief set free
stillness fills the hole
yet my soul unquenched
familiar with sorrow
begs for more tears
to drown out tomorrow

The Anchor of Truth

I unchain my hands to write
for my soul would drown
without the flow of my pen
finding new strokes
to combat menacing undercurrents

I anchor myself with truth
whilst the tide recedes
giving safe passage to shore

Stuck in the Middle

Claiming entitlement
to privileges not bestowed,
you keep jokers to the right.
They serve your needs.
Point your finger to the left;
the clown has paid her dues.

You ignore the 'X'
where buried treasure lies.
My brown-eyed girl,
unwilling to enter
the sacred place,
known as 'middle ground'.

BRAVE

Be the first in a generation

Not to join the masquerade,

Don't creep with the clover

Or dance with the daisies,

Remove yourself

From the hold

Of poison ivy

To reveal your truth;

A valiant sunflower

In a field of glory.

A Mother's Lullaby

Come, rest your weary head
in the warm fold of my bosom,
surrender your anguish,
let stifled tears flow.

The Lighthouse

Lightning strikes

• Once,

• Twice,

• Three times

Yet the lighthouse still stands

• Weather-beaten

• Withered

• Weary

Its fading light

A beacon of hope

To lost souls

Mirage

I see you through fog misted glass
three shadows blurred around the edges.
Sun catches the crystal
blinding my vision,
highlighting the grimy smears.
I strain to keep you in focus
but you are fading.
I wipe the dirt,
my hand heavy with shame,
but you still don't appear;
my mind was playing tricks.
Was it a mirage?
The glass remains cloudy.
I step outside
to the lonely space where you once stood,
and discover:
the glass was dirty on the outside.

Candle

The voile billows
as the flame dances
to the shrill song of the fife.
It's cold icy breath
wrangles with the wick
until stillness resumes.

A flicker of light
rekindles the flame-
languid,
but as yet,
unextinguished.

The Source

Provocative strikes
From behind a thin veil
Infiltrating our senses

Limited awareness
Amidst the bloodshed
As the tributary of blame flows

I blame you
You blame me
I blame myself

But the river is not ours to claim
For the source came from higher ground
The headwater of family

The Swamp

Breaking the toxic cycle
I freed my chains
Leaving them in the swamp
Where no truth remains

A lifetime of judgements
Stain a vulnerable mind
Transitioning adults
A new generation to blind

An invisible army guards
With tongues of fire
My precious jewels
Their tokens to admire

As I float away
On a feather of sorrow
I grieve for my children
Who know not of tomorrow

Where times passes by
As they seal their own fate
With a fraudulent love
Based on deceit and hate

But should deliverance come
Have no thoughts of regret
For love is the truth
With no knowledge of debt

My lullaby waits
In the call of a dove
My love floating down
From a feather above.

Peace

From seeds of righteousness
a battle commences.
Words of anger.
Heartbreak.
Loss.

A mother's surrender,
for it is time to return
her borrowed gift.
Loved.
Free.

Twinkle Twinkle Little Star...

Twinkle one vanished
   in the blink of an eye

Twinkle two exploded
   trails of dust scorching the sky

Leaving little star lonely
   her light growing dim
      the world left in darkness
         as gravity pulls her in

         An abyss of grief
         cries out from my soul
         mourning three stars
         swallowed by a black hole

         I stand in the shadows
         on the dark side of the moon
         not a diamond in sight
         as I hum a hushed tune...

         Twinkle, twinkle, little star
         how I wonder what you are...

A Mother's Prayer for her Children

I pray that when the day comes,
    whilst being the mother you want to be,
      you succeed in becoming
        the mother your children want you to be.

May you prosper and flourish
    with happiness and love in abundance,
    remaining humble and meek,
      and always following *the golden rule.*

Acknowledgements

Alison Williams – Editor.

Sue Burge – Poet. Thank you for the inspiration of your many creative workshops and beautiful collections of work that have taught me so much.

Kate Drakely – wonderful poet friend, who has inspired and supported me with my writing.

Joris van Leeuwen – Cutting Edge Studio. Thanks to you and your team for the superb cover design and formatting of this book.

Martin Rodwell – long suffering husband who listens to my work at any hour of the day, and makes the world worth living in.

Author

Nikki Rodwell is a multi-genre writer. Her debut book 'Catch Me if I Fall' won best-seller status with Amazon and has led to her becoming an advocate for mental health.
She is currently writing a new fiction novel to be released in 2023 and plans to continue with poetry in the foreseeable future.
Find out more on her website:
www.nikkirodwell.co.uk

Printed in Great Britain
by Amazon